Draw Your
PET!

You Can Draw

Dogs!

Katie Dicker

Gareth Stevens
Publishing

Please visit our website, www.garethstevens.com. For a free color catalog of all our high-quality books, call toll free 1-800-542-2595 or fax 1-877-542-2596.

Library of Congress Cataloging-in-Publication Data

Dicker, Katie.
 You can draw dogs! / Katie Dicker.
    pages cm — (Draw your pet!)
 Includes index.
ISBN 978-1-4339-8732-8 (pbk.)
ISBN 978-1-4339-8733-5 (6-pack)
ISBN 978-1-4339-8731-1 (library binding)
1. Dogs in art—Juvenile literature. 2. Drawing—Technique—Juvenile literature. I. Title.
 NC783.8.D64D53 2013
 743.6'9772—dc23

2012022952

Published in 2013 by
Gareth Stevens Publishing
111 East 14th Street, Suite 349
New York, NY 10003

© 2013 Gareth Stevens Publishing

Produced for Gareth Stevens by Calcium Creative Ltd
Illustrated by Mike Lacey
Designed by Paul Myerscough
Edited by Sarah Eason and Harriet McGregor

Photo credits: Dreamstime: Roughcollie 22t; Shutterstock: AnetaPics 10t, 26t, Dien 18, Joe Gough 24, Konstantin Gushcha 20, Eric Isselée cover, 8, 12, 22, 28, Jagodka 26, Alexia Khruscheva 14, Eduard Kyslynskyy 14t, Erik Lam 6, Valeriy Lebedev 18t, Nejron Photo 10, Tanatat 6t, Nikolai Tsvetkov 16b.

Printed in the United States of America

CPSIA compliance information: Batch CW13GS: For further information contact Gareth Stevens, New York, New York at 1-800-542-2595.

Contents

You Can Draw Dogs!

If you love dogs, you'll love to draw them, too! Dogs are loyal, loving, and lots of fun. This makes them one of the most popular of all pets for many children.

There are many different types of dog breed. Some dogs, such as retrievers, are large, muscly animals. Other dogs, such as Yorkshire terriers, are small, dainty dogs. Some dogs need a lot of exercise. Others need only occasional walks. Some dogs are high-strung, while other dogs are playful. In this book, we'll teach you how to care for dogs—and how to draw them, too.

Discover how to draw dogs!

🐾 Follow the steps that show you how to draw each type of dog. Then draw from a photograph of your own pet to create a special pet portrait!

🐾 You Will Need:

• Art paper and pencils

• Eraser

• Coloring pens and/or paints and a paintbrush

🐾 Yorkshire terriers

🐾 dalmations

🐾 boxers

🐾 golden retrievers

🐾 German shepherds

🐾 beagles

Golden Retrievers

One of the most popular of American pet dogs, the golden retriever is loyal and loving. These dogs are smart and respond quickly to commands. Golden retrievers are very patient with children, which makes them a great family pet.

Golden retrievers are many shades of yellow.

Step 1

First, draw the dog's outline. As you draw, pay attention to the proportions of the dog's body.

Step 2

Now add some detailed lines to your picture. Pencil the outline of the fur on the body. Then add the head, ears, legs, and the dog's tail.

Step 3

Lightly pencil the features of the dog's face. Then go over the features with a heavier pencil line.

Caring for your Retriever

🐾 Adult retrievers are very strong and may easily pull you over when on a lead. Take time to train your dog as a puppy. Your pet will then follow your commands when it is fully grown.

🐾 Be sure to walk your dog every day. Retrievers may chew furniture and other objects if they do not get enough exercise. Walking stops chewing!

🐾 Retrievers love to swim. If you take your dog to the beach, it will love playing fetch in the water.

Retriever puppies can be shy around people until they are used to them.

Step 4

Draw lots of fine pencil lines to add shade to the picture. Shade the dog's head, ears, body, legs, and tail. Then draw claws on the paws.

Step 5

Now you can complete your picture by adding color. Use a light brown color for some of the dog's fur. Add depth with a dark brown shade. Color the nose black and the eyes a rich brown.

Beagles

Beagles are sturdy dogs. Their fur is made up of very short hairs, which makes them easy to groom and keep clean. Beagles love to be around people and are very friendly animals. These dogs are loving and loyal to their owners and make great animal friends.

The beagle holds its strong, firm tail high in the air.

Step 1

Draw the outline for your dog. Notice how the dog's tail is held high behind it and how its paws are squarely placed on the ground.

Step 2

Pencil the ears, the shape of the nose and jaw, and the claws on the dog's paws. Draw the outline of its belly.

Step 3

Now draw your dog's nose, muzzle, and eyes. Add some light shading strokes to the chest and rear legs.

🐾 Beagles have minds of their own!
You will need to train your dog thoroughly
to make sure it obeys your commands.

🐾 Beagles have a great sense of smell and can track
a scent for miles. Buy your dog animal scents so
that you can play tracking and chasing games
with it.

🐾 Only let your dog off the lead where it is safe and
where it cannot run too far away. Beagles may
run off if they smell the scent of another animal.

Beagles are hunting dogs, but if trained correctly, they can be very gentle around other pets.

Step 4

Add more detail by shading the tail and back. Draw the outline of the dog's pattern on its body and head.

Step 5

Color your dog to complete it. Choose a palette of rich browns and black for the fur. Finally, add shading with a soft gray color.

German Shepherds

The German shepherd is very strong and muscly. These dogs are often used as police dogs because they are very brave and respond well to commands. German shepherds are very smart and love to learn quickly. This makes them very easy dogs to train.

The German shepherd usually has a black nose and black markings on its head and body.

Step 1

Draw the outline of your dog. Complete the head carefully to make sure you include the dog's tall ears.

Step 2

Pencil the outline of the dog's face. Draw the two paws so that one overlays the other. Pencil the claws. Add some more detailed lines to the body and tail.

Step 3

Add shading to the ears and chest. Pencil the dog's eyes and nose. Notice how the eyes are large and round in shape.

Caring for your German Shepherd

🐾 German shepherds have a strong instinct to protect their owners. This makes them great guard dogs. However, you must handle your dog firmly and let it know that you are the boss. If your pet becomes aggressive around strangers, you can then command it to back down.

🐾 Make sure that you give your dog plenty of exercise. German shepherds are very active and need a lot of mental and physical exercise. Play frisbee with your dog—it will love it!

🐾 Brush your dog every day. German shepherds lose hair daily and need regular grooming.

German shepherds have tall ears that face forward and can stand upright on their heads.

Step 4

Use lots of fine pencil strokes to now add shading and depth to your picture. With a thick-tipped pencil, carefully shade the nose.

Step 5

Add color with a palette of dark grays, black, and chestnut brown. Carefully color the face with a light gray along the center of the nose. Blend the gray into black along the edges of the nose and muzzle.

Yorkshire Terriers

Yorkshire terriers are very small dogs that usually grow just 6 to 7 inches (15 to 17.5 cm) in height and weigh around 7 pounds (3.2 kg). Yorkshire terriers have long, glossy hair. This makes them popular show dogs. For competitions, owners decorate the hair of their pet with cute accessories such as bows!

The hair of a Yorkshire terrier may reach all the way to the ground.

Step 1

Draw your Yorkshire terrier from the side. You can add the rough lines of the fur on the tail and chest. Notice the outline of the bow on the dog's head.

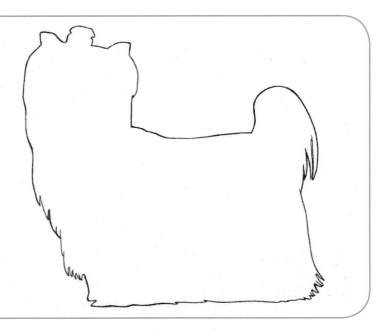

Step 2

Use long pencil lines to draw the fur on the dog's tail, body, and around its head.

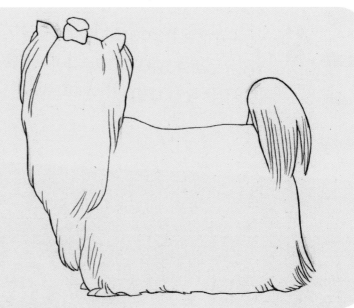

Step 3

Pencil the eyes, nose, and muzzle. Draw the detail of the bow. Add more long lines for the fur around the dog's muzzle.

Caring for your Yorkshire Terrier

🐾 Your pet can become very nervous and may "yap" unless it is kept calm. Don't get it too excited!

🐾 Your dog will need a lot of grooming. You can keep its hair under control by cutting it short. If you like to keep your dog's hair long, make sure you groom it regularly by washing and brushing the coat.

🐾 Yorkshire terriers do not do well in cold conditions. Your dog may need to wear a coat on walks in winter to keep it warm and avoid chills.

Yorkshire terrier puppies are tan and black in color.

Step 4

Add lots of fine lines along the top of the dog's back. Do the same at the base of the dog's fur. Shade the nose and ears.

Step 5

Color your drawing with a palette of dark grays, black, and brown. Paint the bow pink and add white highlights to the fur.

Dalmations

The dalmation is best known as a star of the movie *101 Dalmations*! These dogs are also famous for their beautiful coats, which are white with black spots. Dalmations are lively dogs with a fun, playful character.

Dalmations need plenty of exercise. Be sure to take your dog on regular, daily walks.

Step 1

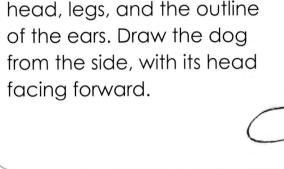

First, draw the outline for your dalmation. Draw the body, head, legs, and the outline of the ears. Draw the dog from the side, with its head facing forward.

Step 2

Add the dog's collar and its jaw. Then draw the claws and markings on the paws. Add light shading to the chest.

Step 3

Pencil the features of the dalmation's face. Add shading to its ears and more shading on the body of the dog.

Caring for your Dalmation

🐾 Exercise your pet regularly. A daily walk between 30 or 40 minutes is best.

🐾 Do not leave your dog alone for long periods of time. Dalmations love to be around people.

🐾 Many dalmations are deaf in one ear. Get to know your pet and make sure it can hear you.

🐾 If you buy a dalmation puppy, take time to train it properly. Young dalmations need lots of attention and can tear up a home if not house-trained.

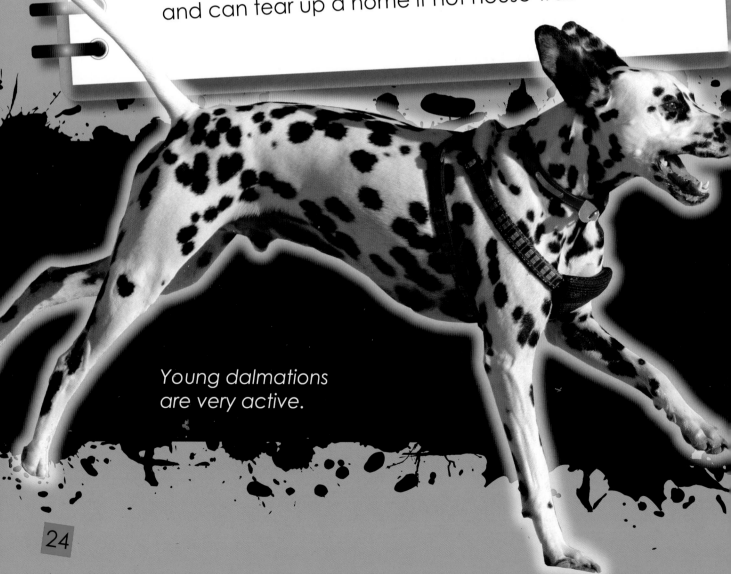

Young dalmations are very active.

Step 4

With a fine-tipped pencil, add the spotted pattern on the dalmation's coat. You can also add some heavier lines of shading.

Step 5

Finish your picture by coloring it. Use a black and gray paint to color the pattern on the fur and the nose, ears, and eyes. Give your dog a brown jaw and dark brown eyes. Use gray to add more shading to the body.

Boxers

Boxers have a powerful, solid-looking body. They also have a short muzzle with a very blunt tip. Boxers are playful, fun-loving dogs and get along well with children. They love to be around people and make a great family pet.

Boxers have short hair and a very stiff tail that is held high above the body.

Step 1

Draw your boxer with its head raised up, looking alert. The tail is held up behind the body and the dog's forelegs are stretched out in front of its body.

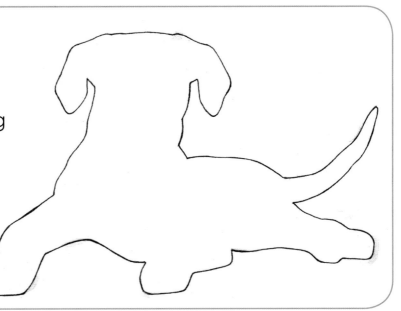

Step 2

Draw the claws and pads at the front of the dog's paws. Add the lines of the muzzle and complete the outline of the boxer's ears.

Step 3

Pencil the features of your dog's face. Include the folds of the skin above its eyes and around its muzzle. Add light shading strokes to the chest and belly.

- Boxers are easy to keep clean. They have short hair that needs to be brushed just once a week.

- Take your boxer on regular daily walks. A boxer that doesn't get enough exercise can become high-strung and difficult to control.

- Play lots of games with your pet—boxers love to have fun. Try fetch or frisbee.

- Only bathe your boxer when it is necessary. Some boxers love to roll in poop when out on a walk. If you have a poop-loving boxer, you'll need to give your messy dog a bath more often!

All boxers have huge, chocolate-brown eyes.

Step 4

To create the dark markings around the eyes and on the muzzle, shade the dog's face with a thick-tipped pencil. Use a fine-tipped pencil for the lighter shading on the body.

Step 5

Complete your picture with color. Use a palette of chestnut brown, gray, and black. Add white highlights on the chest, tail, legs, and face.

Glossary

accessories: bows, ribbons, and other objects added to an outfit to make it look pretty

aggressive: will attack quickly

blunt: flat, not curved

command: message or signal that tells a dog what to do

competition: dog show in which different breeds of dog are shown off by their owners in the hope that they will win a prize

deaf: unable to hear

detail: the fine lines and small features of a picture

groom: to care for a dog by brushing it, washing it, and clipping its nails

guard dog: a dog that protects people and property

high-strung: nervous, easily frightened

house-trained: when an animal is trained so that it can live in a house without destroying it

instinct: a natural, unthinking desire to do something

loyal: to be true to or devoted to someone

muzzle: the snout or nose and mouth of a dog

palette: a range of colors

proportion: the size of one part of the body in relation to another

respond: to react to something

scent: the smell given off by a living creature

shading: pencil strokes that add depth to a picture

show dog: dog that is shown in competitions

sturdy: solid, not easily knocked over

track: to follow the trail of something by following the scent it leaves behind

For More Information

Books

Hodge, Susie. *How to Draw Dogs in Simple Steps*. Tunbridge Wells, UK: Search Press, 2010.

Rosen, Michael. J. *My Dog!: A Kids' Guide to Keeping a Happy and Healthy Pet*. New York, NY: Workman Publishing Company, 2011.

Stacey, Nolon. *Dogs and Puppies*. Irvine, CA: Walter Foster Publishing, 2011.

Zobel, Derek. *Caring For Your Dog*. Minneapolis, MN: Bellwether Media, 2010.

Websites

Find out more about different kinds of dogs and how to look after them at:
www.canismajor.com/dog

Discover lots of different dog breeds at:
www.enchantedlearning.com/subjects/mammals/dog/index.shtml

Visit the website of the American Kennel Club to find out more about caring for dogs:
www.akc.org/kids_juniors/index.cfm?nav_area=kids%20juniors

Publisher's note to educators and parents: Our editors have carefully reviewed these websites to ensure that they are suitable for students. Many websites change frequently, however, and we cannot guarantee that a site's future contents will continue to meet our high standards of quality and educational value. Be advised that students should be closely supervised whenever they access the Internet.

Index